Dirty Dog

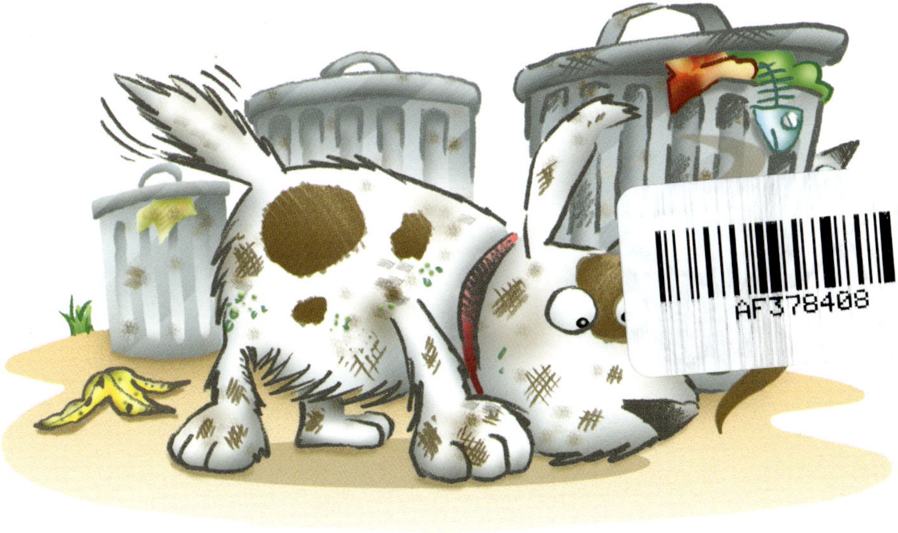

Claire Llewellyn
Illustrated by Beccy Blake

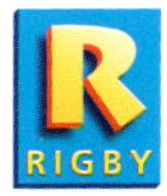

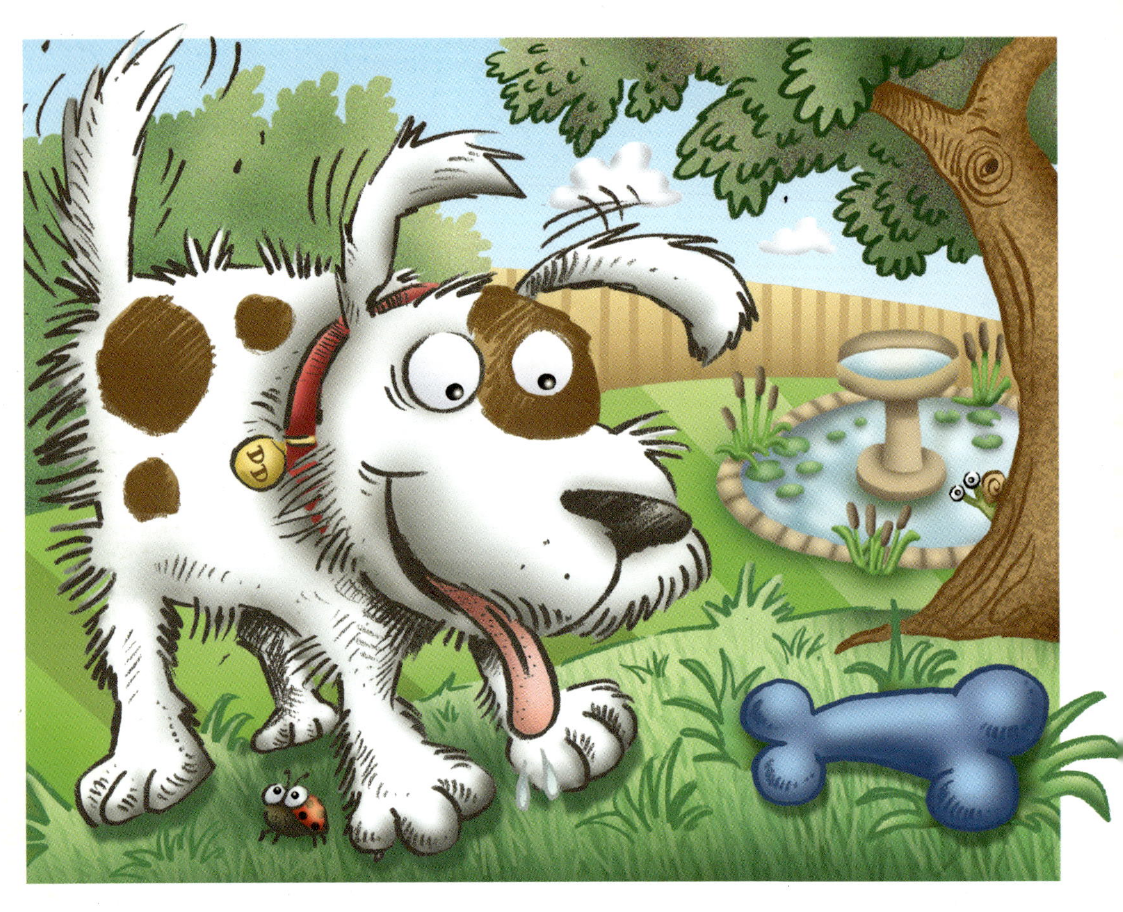

Dirty Dog sees a bone.

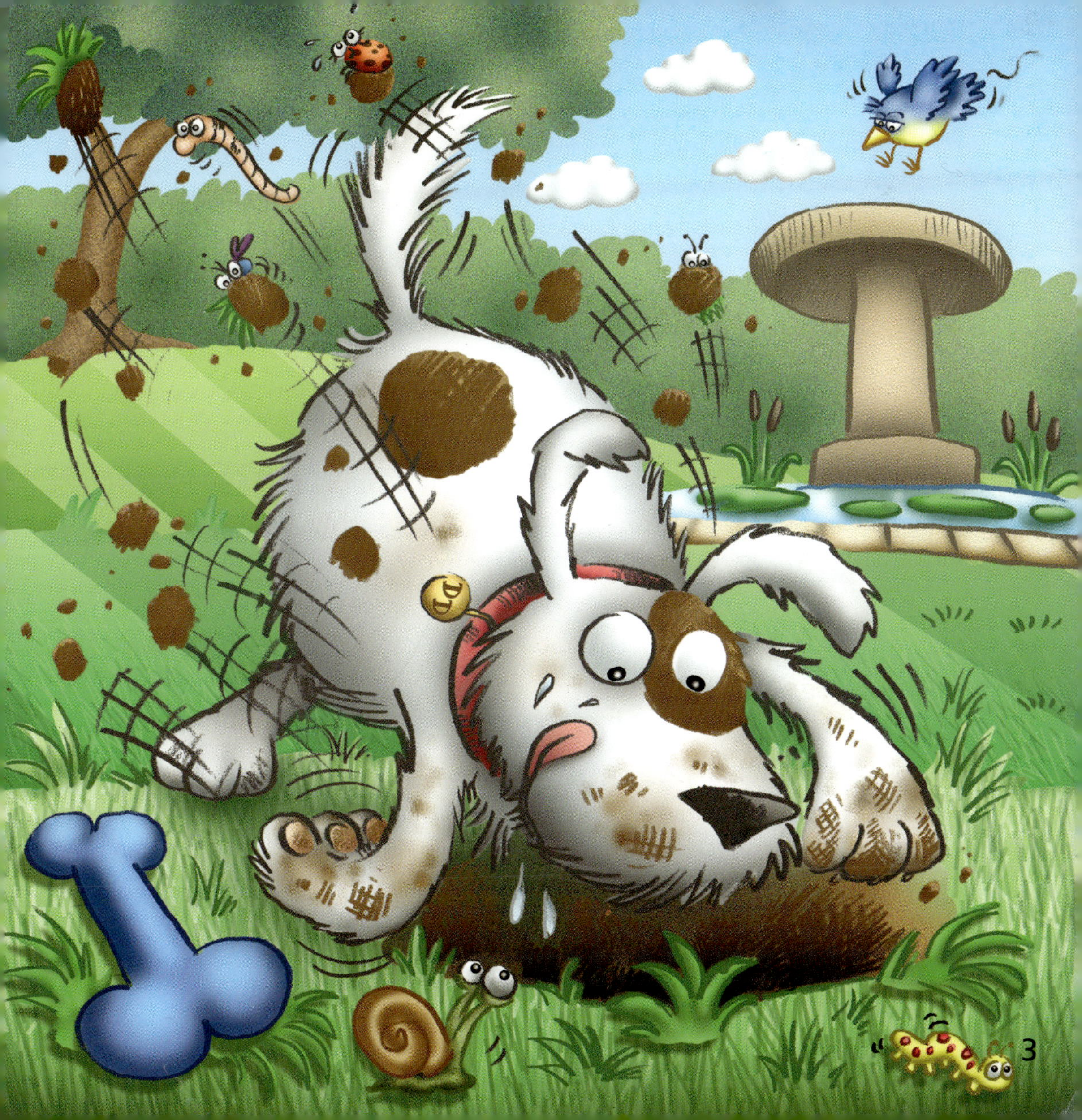

3

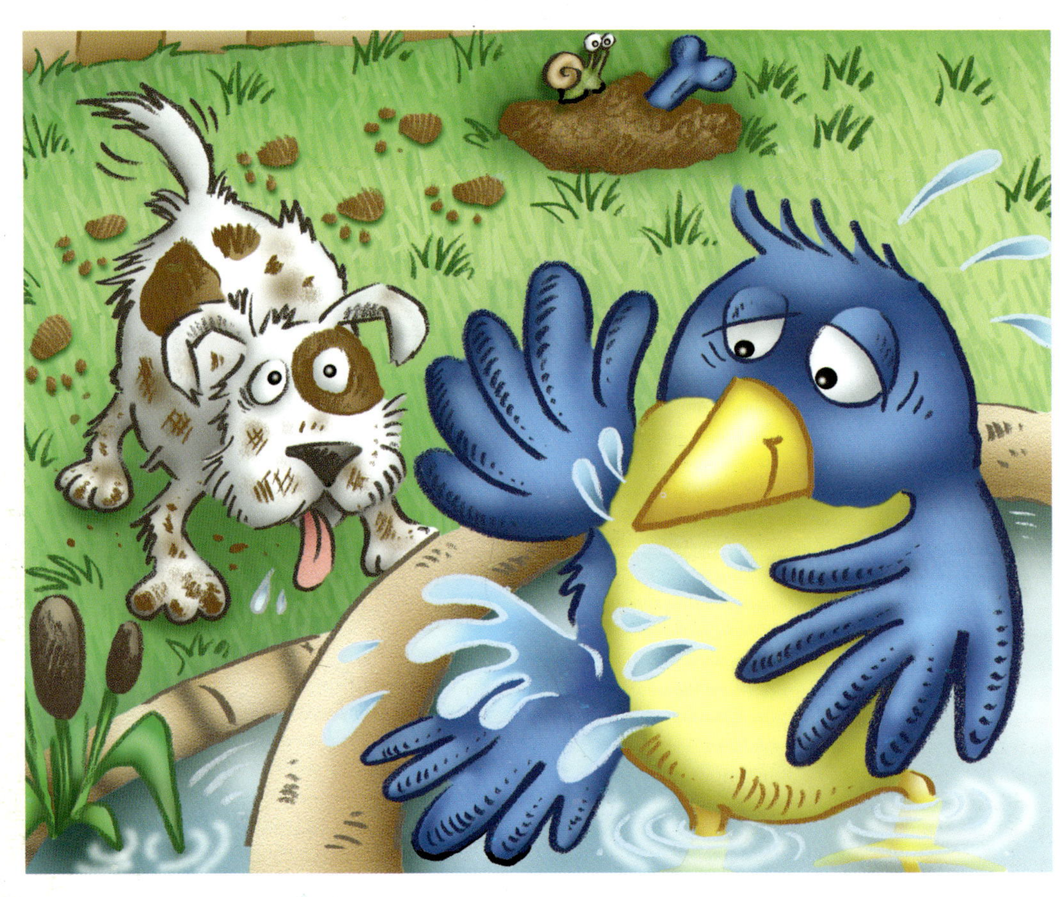

Dirty Dog sees a bird.

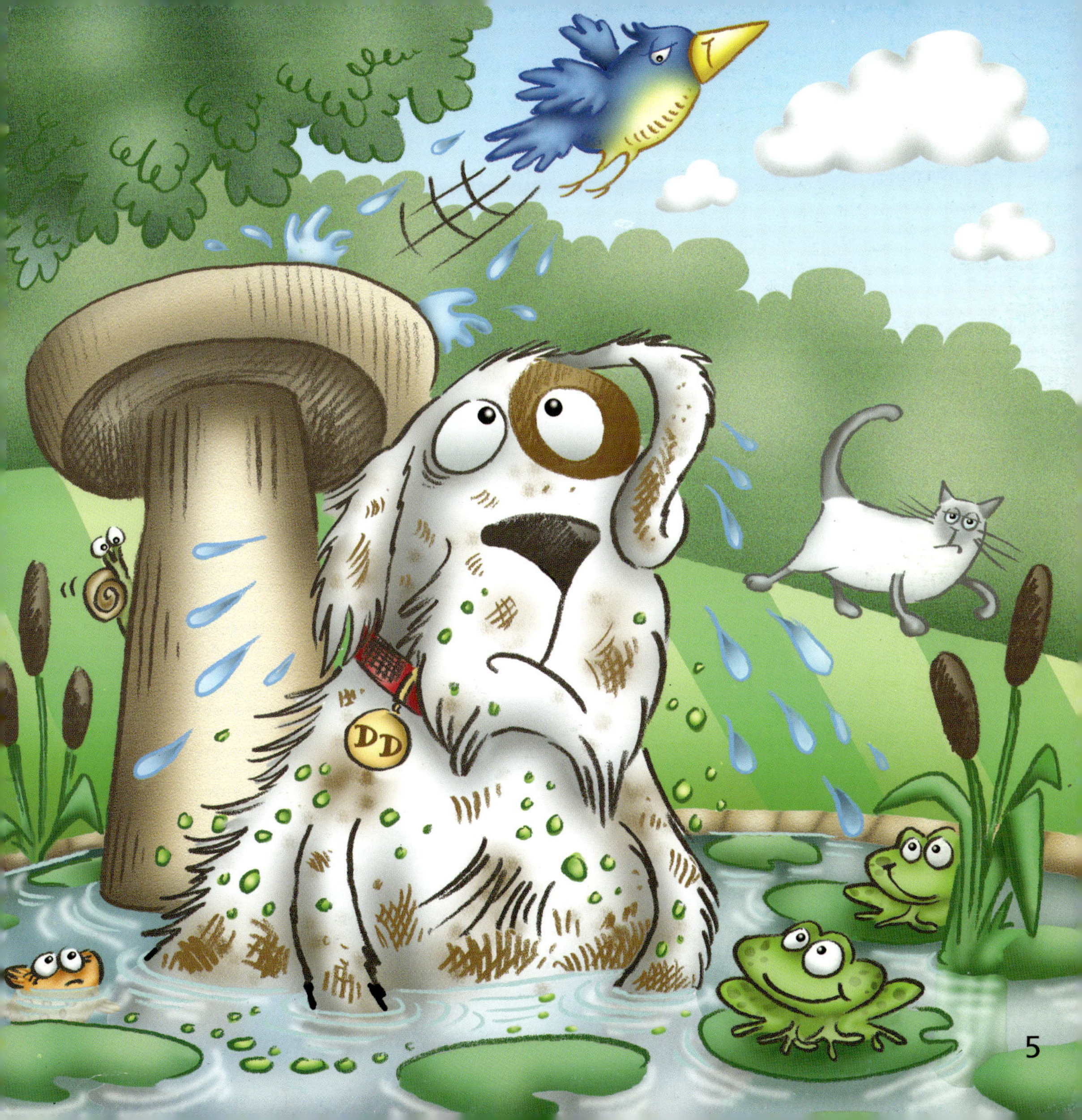

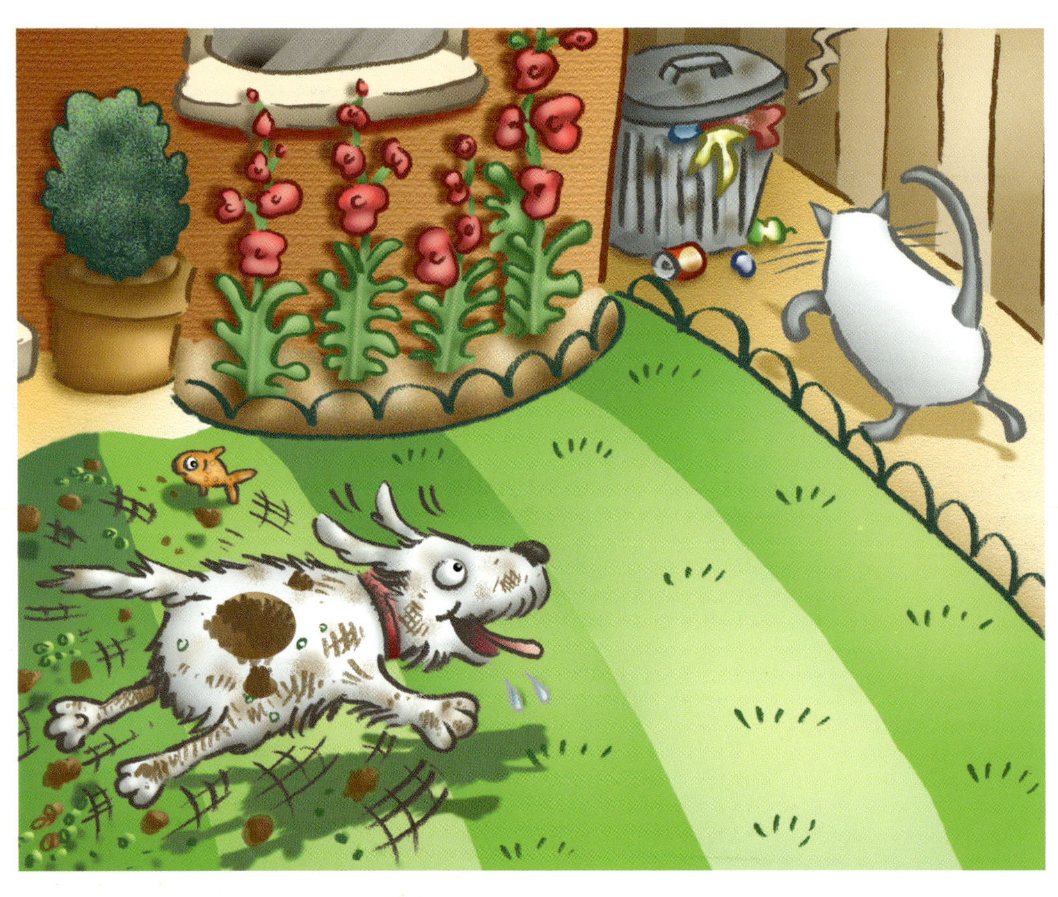

Dirty Dog sees a cat.

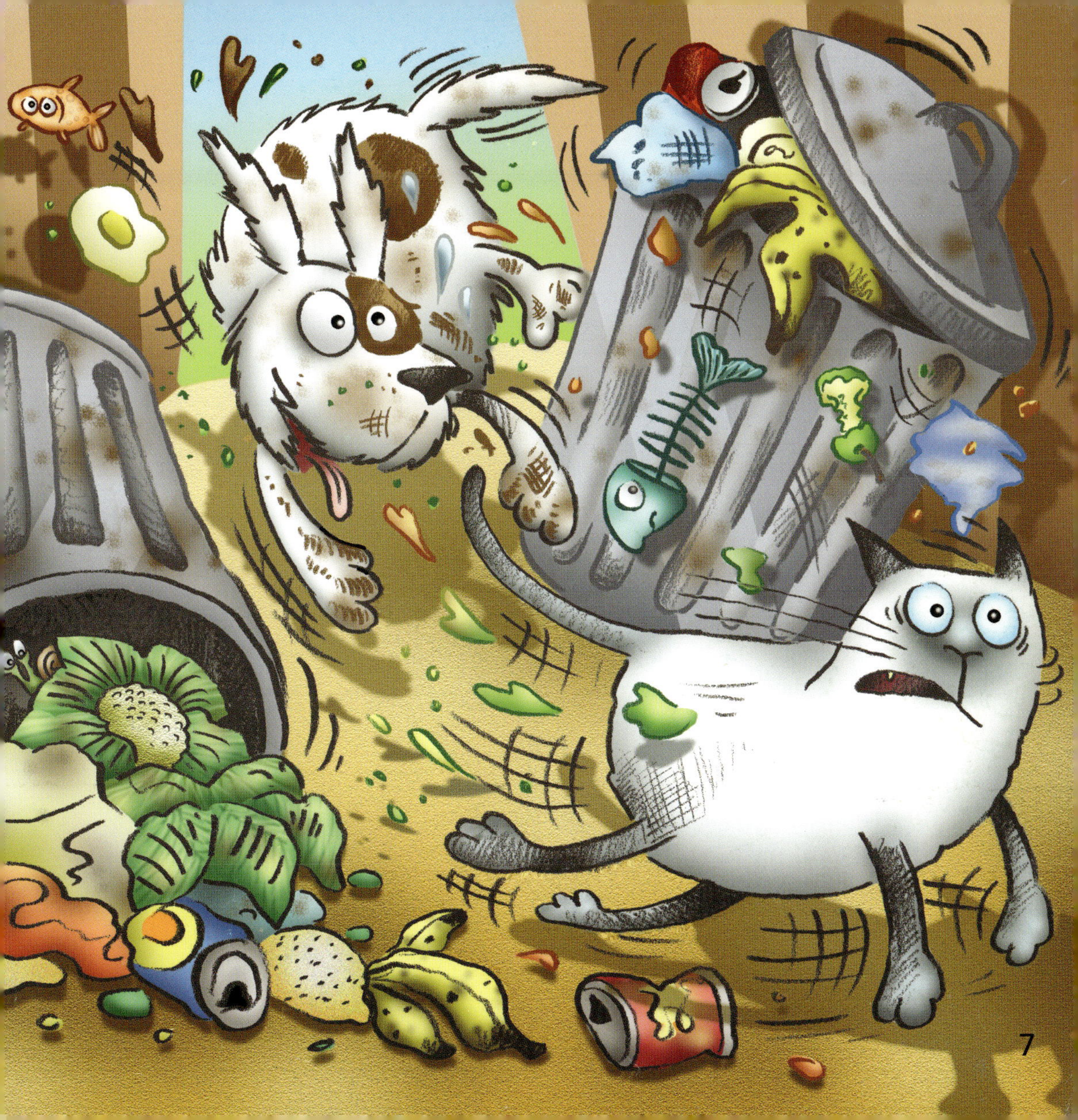

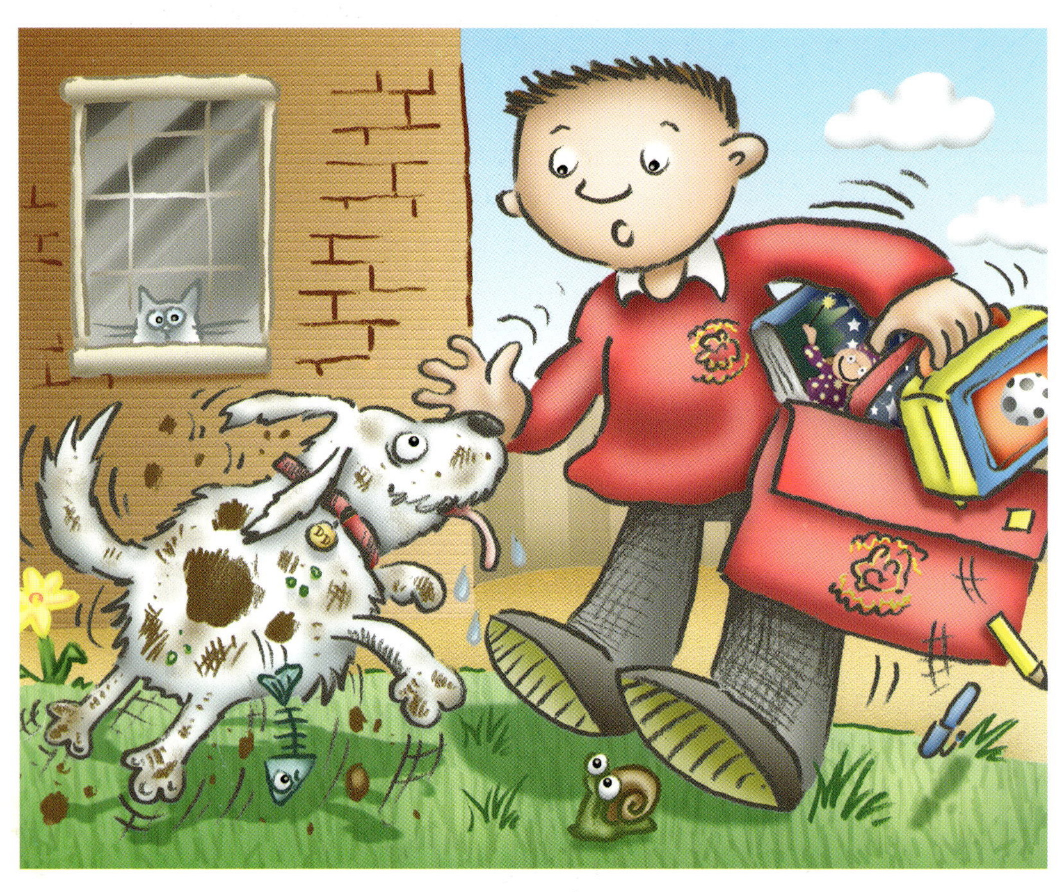

Dirty Dog sees me!